DIVORCE
AND YOUR FAMILY™

A TEEN'S GUIDE TO CUSTODY

TIMOTHY CALLAHAN AND CLAUDIA ISLER

ROSEN
PUBLISHING®
New York

Published in 2017 by The Rosen Publishing Group, Inc.
29 East 21st Street, New York, NY 10010

First Edition

Library of Congress CataloginginPublication Data

Names: Callahan, Timothy.
Title: A teen's guide to custody / Timothy Callahan and Claudia Isler.
Description: New York : Rosen Publishing, 2017. | Series: Divorce and your family|
Includes index.
Identifiers: ISBN 9781508171300 (library bound)
Subjects: LCSH: Divorce--Juvenile literature. | Custody of children--Juvenile
literature. | Children of divorced parents--Juvenile literature.
Classification: LCC HQ777.5 C35 2017 | DDC 306.89--dc23

Manufactured in China

CONTENTS

INTRODUCTION

When divorce occurs in a family, everyone is affected. Even though divorce is the dissolution of a marriage, it's not just the married couple's relationship that's changing. If the couple are parents, it also means the end of their family as it was. Although parents continue to be parents, no matter their marital status, the lives of their children will be altered forever after a divorce.

Around 40 percent of all marriages in the United States end in divorce. Every year, more than 1.5 million children are affected by divorce. For many teenagers, divorce is a part of their lives. Divorce doesn't have to affect your life in negative ways, but be prepared for a lot of change.

When your parents get divorced, the first thing you must face is how your family has suddenly changed and, in most cases, been rearranged. Because your parents will no longer want to live together, chances are one will move out of your home. Maybe everyone will move out of the home because it is too expensive under the new circumstances. You may even find yourself living in a different town, attending a new school. Most likely, you will

Divorce comes with a lot of change. One of the biggest changes is figuring out your role in the new version of your family. You might feel like the rope in a game of tug-of-war between your parents.

live most of the time with one parent and visit your other parent on weekends or during school vacations. You will have to adapt to shuttling back and forth and to not seeing your parents as often as you once did.

This new life may seem strange and confusing, and you may feel as though you don't even have a family anymore. Divorce comes with a whole range of emotions. Often, young people whose parents are divorcing feel as though they are caught in the middle. Their family is breaking apart, and they aren't sure where they belong.

No matter what the future holds, you will always have a family. It will simply look different from the way it once did. The word "family" means different things to different people. Some teens live with only one parent, some live with both their mom and their dad, and some live in foster homes. Other teens split time between two homes, and some have stepparents, stepsiblings, and half siblings. These are all families; they're just made up of different people.

One of the most important issues that divorcing couples must agree on is custody. The parent who has custody of you cares and supervises you on a daily basis. There are a variety of custody options that divorcing couples choose or are awarded by a judge.

If you do feel caught in the middle of your parents' divorce, afraid of what it means for you, then you will find this resource very helpful. It will explain the custody process, how decisions are made, and how these decisions will affect your life. It will give you advice on dealing with your parents, the court system, and your own difficult and confused emotions. Divorce isn't the end of the world, although it can sometimes feel like it. You will survive your parents' divorce. And you may even be a stronger and happier person for it.

That may sound strange now; it might take a few years to find some truth in it. Chances are, your parents were not happy in their marriage. If they fought a lot or one parent stayed away to avoid the other, you might welcome the change. It is better to see your parents happy and thriving, and often times, divorce, however painful the process may be, can allow unhappy parents to blossom. You might find that after the dust settles, you are a lot happier, too.

CHAPTER ONE

WHEN YOU LIVE WITH ONE PARENT ALL THE TIME

One of the decisions made during your parents' divorce regarded custody. This was a determination of who would care for you, where you would live, and how often you would see each parent.

You may end up living with one parent all the time. That parent has sole custody of you. Sole custody means that only one of your parents or your guardian makes all the decisions that will affect your life. These include where you'll live; where you'll go to school; your religious education, if any; which doctors will check on your health; what time you need to be home for dinner; and just about everything else.

When Hayley's parents got divorced, they promised her that things wouldn't change too much. But Hayley's dad moved out, and then Hayley's mom rented a smaller place for just the two of them in a new town. Hayley lives with her mom and sees her dad a lot, but things have definitely changed. "It's weird not to have Dad at the dinner table every night," says Hayley. "Mom and Dad always talked about everything. If I wanted to go out with my friends or to a party, they would discuss it before telling me I could or couldn't go. Now it's just Mom telling me what to do all the time."

The Custodial Parent

The parent who has sole custody and has all these responsibilities is called the custodial parent. Most of the time, the custodial parent has physical custody of you. This means that you live

Chances are, you will live with your custodial parent most of the time. You will visit and stay with your noncustodial parent as your parents and the courts have agreed, usually on weekends and during some school breaks.

with him or her. The custodial parent may receive child support payments, either weekly or monthly, from the noncustodial parent. The parent who doesn't have custody of you is called the noncustodial parent. Child support is money to help pay for your clothes, food, transportation, and any other expenses of day-to-day living. Your custodial parent is legally required to spend this money on the things you need, such as visits to the dentist and school supplies.

Sometimes your custodial parent will receive additional money, called alimony. This money is intended to help support your parent, who may have trouble making ends meet now that he or she is on his or her own. The money may go toward the rent or mortgage, food, and clothing. The custodial parent does not receive this money automatically. The court decides whether your parent will receive alimony and if so, how much is appropriate. The court also chooses an appropriate amount for child support payments if your parents cannot agree on what is reasonable. The amount of money is different from one family to the next, depending on each family's financial situation. Laws about alimony and who should receive it are different from one state to the next.

When a Court Must Decide

Hopefully your parents will agree on who should have sole custody of you without needing the court's help. The court and your parents are required to make a decision that is in your best interest. This means that you must live where you will be taken care of best and, as a result, where you'll be happier. Maybe your mom goes to school full time, works late hours at her job, or has a job that takes her out of town frequently. In that case, chances are, you'll live with your dad, simply because he's home more often and has more time to give you.

Sometimes parents disagree about who should take care of you. In these cases, the court must make the decision for them. There are other factors the court will consider besides how much time your parents have to spend with you. Some of these are a parent's history of physical or emotional abuse, if any; whether there is a history of drug or alcohol abuse; and whether there is another adult involved with whom your parent may be having a romantic relationship.

Older kids, especially teens, often get to talk with the judge and a social worker about where they would be most comfortable. A social worker is a person whose job it is to make sure you're taken care of after the divorce. Your opinion may not determine the final decision, but it will help. If there's something you need to say, make sure you say it. Custody decisions are about your best interests, so your vote matters. Custody decisions can change, too, and they can be reviewed periodically.

The Noncustodial Parent's Role

Just because one parent is in charge of daily decisions does not mean that you'll never see your other parent. If you live with your mom, it's likely that you'll still see your dad. The only situation in which you wouldn't see your noncustodial parent is when that parent may be a danger to you. If your mom or dad has a history of drug abuse or has abused you physically or sexually, the court may keep that parent away from you to protect you.

In most cases, though, your parent will be given visitation rights. Visitation rights are a legal privilege given to the noncustodial parent to see his or her children regularly. This is your time

Visitation allows you to spend time with your noncustodial parent. Because you don't live with him or her most of the time, you will want to make the most of your time together.

with your mom or dad. Visitations often have a specific schedule, such as every other weekend, half the summer, or on specific holidays. Some parents, for example, have Wednesday nights and school vacations with their children. Visitations can be different for every family.

Visitation is different for everybody because your parents need to work out a schedule that works best for them and for

You may be asked to weigh in on custody during your parents' divorce proceedings. You will not have to say anything that will hurt your parents. Rather, you will be given the opportunity to state a preference, if you have one.

you. Sometimes parents can't agree on the schedule, so the court makes the decision about what is best for you based on information it has about your and your parents' schedules. Even if you're with your mom all week, you're probably both pretty busy with work and school. On the weekend, your mom might like to spend time with you doing relaxing things like going to the

movies, visiting the park, or even just hanging out together. She may want your father to have you every other weekend so that he can have some fun time with you, too.

It's important for you to let your parents know what arrangements make you comfortable. Getting your feelings out in the open may help you feel better, and it may help to change things you're not happy with.

Do I Have a Say?

In all this discussion of your parents, you may wonder what your rights are. Your parents and the court are responsible for making custody decisions that are in your best interest. According to the United Nations' Declaration of the Rights of the Child, you are entitled to a childhood without adult responsibilities, a happy family life, a decent education at a school that addresses your learning needs, a doctor who knows you, a safe neighborhood to live in, and a chance to succeed in life. These are issues that your parents and the court will also look at, in addition to your physical and emotional safety.

The court may ask for your opinion, depending on your age. Not every state in the United States has the same laws. Some give preference to your desires, meaning they take into account what it is that you want, but others don't.

You may be assigned a lawyer, particularly if your parents can't agree on visitation rights or where you'll live and go to school.

Be sure to tell your lawyer how you feel about these issues and why. If your opinion is going to influence the judge, this is the way to get it out there before decisions are made. This doesn't mean, however, that your lawyer will automatically do and say everything you tell her. And most kids do not get lawyers. But it's important not to feel guilty about looking out for yourself. If there is a good reason why you should live with one parent and not the other, tell your lawyer, a social worker (the court can appoint one for you), or even a school guidance counselor.

Even if only one of your parents has physical custody of you, for example, even if you live only with your dad full time, you will still get to see your mom. She'll come to visit you and take you out to do fun things, and sometimes you'll probably get to spend the night at her new place.

Things are not going to be like they were before the divorce, it's true. But you can get used to the changes. Everyone in your family will need time to adjust to all the new demands on time and schedules, but eventually it will work out. And usually, believe it or not, everyone is happier in the end.

CHAPTER TWO

WHEN YOUR PARENTS SHARE YOU

Sole custody isn't the only option for divorced parents. Another type of custody involves a parenting arrangement that is more equally balanced. When a divorce is fairly straightforward, it is called a no-fault divorce. This means neither spouse is considered guilty of breaking the marriage vows. The legal cause is irreconcilable differences, or incompatibility, which means that your parents just cannot get along with each other. The divorce is granted because the marriage is simply over—the couple can no longer live together happily.

In these cases, both parents will want to arrange to see you as much as possible even though they no longer live together. That's where joint custody comes in. Joint custody is simply the awarding of custody to both parents.

Ricki wasn't sure what would become of her when she found out her parents were splitting up. She knew her dad was moving out. Would she have to move in with him if she ever wanted to see him? Or would she stay with her mom, even though her mother traveled often for business? To Ricki's relief, her parents sat her down before her father moved out. They told her they would be sharing custody.

Ricki lived with her mother for one week, then moved across town the next week to live with her dad. She alternated every week with each parent. It was a little confusing at first because she kept forgetting where she was and where she had left certain clothes and books, but she got used to it eventually. According to Ricki, it was all worth it because she got to spend a lot of time with both her mother and her father.

Parents who have joint custody often enlist the help of advisers. While they might have agreed on things informally, now they might meet with mediators, counselors, teachers, and financial planners to plan their childrens' lives.

Joint Custody

Also called shared custody, joint custody can take two forms: joint legal custody and joint physical custody. Joint legal custody means both parents share equally in the decision making regarding the child. Your parents will decide together what time you should be home from the school dance or whether you can go to that concert that all your friends are going to.

Joint physical custody refers to the actual amount of time the child spends with each parent. The time may be limited (such as every other weekend with one parent), or it may be more equal (three days of the week with one parent, four with the other). Joint physical custody may help to keep your relationships with each parent strong, but such an arrangement can sometimes feel unstable. It means you have to be very flexible.

THE MANY KINDS OF CUSTODY

Custody arrangements can more complicated than sole custody and joint custody. Here are some custody assignations and their definitions:

Legal custody: A parent has the right to make important decisions regarding his or her child's welfare.

Physical custody: The parent with whom the child lives has the right to make day-to-day decisions regarding the child's welfare.

Sole custody: One parent alone has legal or physical custody or both

(continued from the previous page)

Joint custody: Parents share legal, physical, or both legal and physical custody.

Joint legal custody: Parents share the authority to make decisions about the child's welfare. They are expected to discuss and agree upon important decisions.

Joint physical custody: The child lives, on a more or less equal-time basis, with both parents. Times might alternate day to day, week to week, or month to month, or the child may be with one parent during the school year and the other during summer vacation. The parent with whom the child spends the greater amount of time may be said to have "primary physical custody," and the other party to have "secondary physical custody."

Split custody: Each parent has physical custody of at least one of the children, usually with alternating weekends and holidays, with the children together at those times.

Bird's nest custody: The children stay in the family home, and the parents take turns moving in and out, in effect visiting the children.

Parents who don't live together have joint custody when they agree, or a court orders them, to share the decision-making responsibilities and/or physical control and custody of their children. Joint custody can exist if the parents are divorced, separated, no longer living together, or even if they never lived together. It's common for couples who share physical custody to share legal custody as well, but not necessarily the other way around.

Moving from Place to Place

Usually, when parents share custody, they work out physical custody according to their schedules and housing arrangements. If

Going from one parent's home to the other's can take a little getting used to. But being away from one parent for a little while can help you appreciate that parent more when you do see him or her.

your parents can't agree, the court will decide on an arrangement. You might split weeks between each parent's house. This is a common compromise. Other possibilities include alternating years or six-month periods or spending weekends and holidays with one parent while spending weekdays with the other.

Joint custody has the advantages of giving you constant contact and involvement with both parents and giving each of your parents a break from being your "only" parent. There are disadvantages, however: you may feel shuttled around, as if you can never just stay in one place. Also, if your parents cannot cooperate with each other, this can affect your daily routine, which may be upsetting. Be sure to talk to your parents about things that are bothering you. You do not need to feel guilty if sometimes you'd like to choose where to stay for the weekend, and your parents will probably let you do what you want when they can.

Joint Legal Custody

There are actually many different types of custody arrangements, and different states have different laws governing them. The most common custody arrangement, however, is joint legal custody. This is when one parent has physical custody and the other parent has "parenting time," or visitation.

There is no specific amount of visitation a court must grant. However, a typical time-split arrangement might look like this: alternate weekends from 6 p.m. Friday to 6 p.m. Sunday; every Wednesday from 5 to 8 p.m.; alternating holidays (New Year's Day, Memorial Day, Independence Day, Labor Day, Thanksgiving, Christmas Eve, Christmas Day, Father's Day, Mother's Day); alternate birthdays; half of school's spring and winter vacations; and four weeks during summer vacation in blocks of two weeks.

Trying to keep track of whose house you're staying at and when, along with all your other activities, can be a challenge. It will help you to keep your own calendar and to coordinate it with your parents.

This arrangement may sound confusing at first, but it is a system that will allow you to see as much of both your parents as possible. It's not the same as having them both in the house together, but it's the next best thing. Be sure you tell your parents if you don't think the arrangement is working or if there is some other schedule that works better for you. They may be willing to be flexible if they think it will make you happier.

CHAPTER THREE

THE INS AND OUTS OF VISITATION

When your parents divorce and custody is decided, you will find yourself "visiting" more than you ever have. What does this mean? Visitation is the time you spend with the noncustodial parent. If your parents have agreed that you will live with your father during the week and stay with your mother on weekends, that time with your mother is called visitation.

Usually, during the custody negotiations, parents—often with the assistance of their lawyers or a judge—agree to a visitation schedule. This is a schedule of weekends, holidays, and school vacations when you and your mom or dad are together. There is no law that says what a visitation schedule should be; they are as individual as the people who use them.

Hakeem felt very strange about the visitation schedule his parents drew up after they got divorced. He missed having everyone living under one roof, and he didn't like to be stuck with such a formal schedule when he wanted to see his mother or his father.

Now he notices that his mother acts too happy and friendly when he visits. She used to get mad at him when he did something wrong, but now she lets a lot of things go. She doesn't feel like the same mother he grew up with.

How Visitation Is Determined

Visitation can seem complicated because so many laws apply, but it's fairly simple in practice. If your mother is given sole custody, your father will be granted visitation rights. If your father is given sole custody, your mother will be granted visitation rights. This means that the noncustodial parent, the one who does not live with you, will be able to see you on a regular basis, with set times and days. Or it may be more flexible, depending on what your parents agree to. The court will examine the terms and, based on what's in your best interests, approve or change them a bit.

No matter what happens, there will be a schedule that your family will follow to make sure that you get to spend time with the parent you don't live with. It will take some getting used to, but after a while you'll probably like the special time you spend with each parent.

Reasonable visitation is when the schedule calls for times and places that make sense and are convenient for everyone involved. Such schedules are generally left to your parents to create. Your parents must cooperate and communicate with each other frequently for this to work.

Sometimes the court making custody decisions sets up the visitation schedule. A schedule designed by the court is called a fixed visitation schedule. The court is more likely to step in and do this if your parents are so angry with each other that constant contact between them could hurt or upset you.

In a situation in which one of your parents is suspected or accused of abuse, an adult other than the custodial parent must

You and your siblings will have a second home with your noncustodial parent. If you've always had your own room, you might need to get used to sharing one with your sibling.

be present at all times during the visit. This is called supervised visitation. That adult may or may not be someone you know. He or she may be someone agreed upon by your parents or someone appointed by the court. Either way, the court must approve that adult.

In some states, visitation is designed specifically to suit the needs of the children, not the parents. In Illinois, for example, a judge can't take away or limit a parent's visitation rights unless he or she finds that it would be dangerous for a child's physical, mental, moral, or emotional health. For instance, if your parent abuses drugs or alcohol, the judge will not want you to have visits with that parent. However, as long as you're safe and happy with your parent, the court will make sure you get to spend time

If your parent is suspected of abuse, your visits with him or her may be supervised by a court-apppointed professional or family member. These supervised visits will continue until the court rules otherwise.

with him or her.

The parent you live with and the parent who has visiting rights often will agree on when and where the visits will take place. But if they don't, the court will decide. The court will consider things like your age, your parents' work schedules, the visiting parent's relationship with you, the home conditions of both parents, and any special problems you or your siblings might have, such as physical or emotional conditions.

Judges will usually try to establish regular weekly or alternating weekend and holiday visitation, with a fair sharing of school vacations and holidays. Also, a parent does not lose the right to visit you because of a failure to pay child support, and a parent can't stop the other from visiting you because of a missed payment.

How to Handle Visitation Successfully

You should be available, or ready to go, at the time agreed upon for visitation. It's your custodial parent's job to make sure that you are ready and have whatever you need for the visit. The visiting parent should arrive on time so as not to keep you waiting (or mess up the custodial parent's schedule). Occasionally, the visitation schedule may need to be changed. If one parent has made plans with you that conflict with visitation rights, your parents should be reasonable and work something out. Your well-being, health, happiness, and safety should be the first concern of both your parents.

If your parent does not show up for a visit and does not notify the other parent, you'll feel rejected. Your parents should make every effort to prevent this, but try to remember that sometimes schedules just don't work out. And think about what it

No matter how disappointed you may be, give your parent a break if he or she misses a visit. Parents make mistakes, just as kids do. However, you can tell your parent that his or her absence made you feel rejected.

was like when your parent was still living with you. Didn't your dad ever have to cancel plans with you? Hasn't your mom ever forgotten to do something with you that you planned? It's not necessarily different now. If one parent repeatedly misses visits, however, it may be time to reassess the visitation schedule. It's not fair for him or her to disappoint and hurt you regularly by missing visits.

Your mom should not use visits to check up on your dad (or vice versa), nor should you be used for this purpose. Visitation is not an opportunity for your parents to continue arguments. The visiting parent should not spend time with you if he or she has been drinking or using drugs. If you think he or she is under the influence of these substances, make sure your custodial parent knows this before you leave the house with your visiting parent.

Your parents should not make wild promises to you about visits they know will not happen. These promises make it hard to trust and respect your parents. You may see your mom or dad making promises he or she can't keep or offering things that he or she can't really afford to buy. After a divorce, a parent often feels as though he or she needs to prove his or her love for you, especially if you don't live with him or her. Make sure your mom or dad knows that you don't love him or her any less just because you're no longer living together. Spending time with your parent means more than anything he or she could ever buy you. Make sure your mom or dad knows this.

Visits should not be limited to where you live. The other parent's home, a day out, or an activity like a picnic or a day at an amusement park, are good alternatives.

Visitation should be a time for you and your parent to enjoy one another. Your parent may bring another person, perhaps an adult friend, along on a visit. If this makes you feel like your parent does not have enough time to give you his or her undivided attention, try to explain how you feel. If that doesn't work, talk to your custodial parent about it. Your parents should both make every effort to discuss and deal with any problems that come up.

OTHER PEOPLE TO VISIT

Visitation isn't limited to parents: a court may grant reasonable visitation privileges, in appropriate circumstances, to grandparents and great-grandparents. Over the past few years, grandparents have begun requesting visits with grandchildren whose parents get divorced. Many states have passed laws allowing grandparents to seek a court order for visits if they've been denied visits by the parents. Some states require that a minimum period of time pass (three to six months) before the visits begin. During this period, everyone can calm down and adjust after the divorce. Other courts require a hearing. If the visits are granted, the court will usually create a schedule that everyone involved is required to follow.

Each case is unique; there is no specific formula for grandparent visitation. This is a fairly new policy and one that does not exist in all states. New York, California, and Arkansas are three of the states that have passed laws giving grandparents the legal right to see their grandchildren. If your mother and stepfather get a divorce, does your former stepfather have any visitation rights? Can you continue to visit him even though he's now legally out of the picture? After a divorce, your stepparent may also want to visit you. You may be very close with a stepfather or stepmother and want him or her to remain a part of your life

(continued from the previous page)

State lawmakers are now considering laws to help parents and kids who find themselves in this situation. Most states, at this time, don't provide step-parents with visitation rights. Some courts, however, will look at the whole picture. The judge will consider how long your stepparent has been involved in your life, your opinion about visitation, and other factors. Courts have granted former stepparents visitation with their stepchildren. Again, the bottom line is what's best for you. Remember, it's all in "the best interests of the child."

When a Parent Veers from the Schedule

Parents may agree to modify, or change, the visitation or even the custody arrangement. This modified agreement, called a stipulated modification, may be made without court approval. If one parent does not stick to the new plan, however, the other will have no legal support to fix the problem. If one parent wants to make changes to the custody arrangements that the other doesn't agree to, the first parent must file a motion (a written request) with the court. Usually, the change will be made only if the parent making the request can demonstrate a "substantial change in circumstances." Substantial changes might be a geographic move or a change in lifestyle, such as a more flexible work schedule or recovery from drug or alcohol abuse.

Sometimes parents get worried or convinced that children belong only with them and not with the former spouse. Occasionally, a parent will break the law in an attempt to protect his or her children or hurt his or her ex-spouse. Visiting parents are not supposed to cross state lines with children without consent from the custodial parent. If you are supposed to see your

If your parent keeps you longer than the visitation agreement allows or takes you somewhere far away without your other parent's permission, he or she may be accused of kidnapping, a serious offense.

mom for the weekend, and she takes you on a trip to an unfamiliar place or a trip that is longer than the weekend, she may be guilty of abducting, or kidnapping, you. The laws that apply to any kidnapper would apply here. If caught, the parent guilty of this crime faces time in jail.

If you think your parent is breaking the visitation agreement, you can try talking to him or her. You can also try to contact your custodial parent. If you can get that parent on the phone, tell him or her where you are and whom you're with. Notify an adult, preferably a police officer, that your parent has broken your visitation agreement. It might seem mean or disloyal to your parent, but he or she has broken the law. Custody arrangements were made with your best interest in mind, and both parents are legally bound to follow them.

Visitation schedules are for your benefit, set up so that you get to spend time with both parents. Like the divorce itself, this schedule will take some getting used to. After a while, it will be as routine as getting up and brushing your teeth. And because the time you spend with each parent has been carefully worked out, it will feel special, like time set aside just for you.

Divorce doesn't end your parents' responsibilities toward you. Each of your parents should try to play a central and important role in your life. Your parents haven't stopped loving you, and they haven't lost interest in you. They each still want and need to show you all the affection and give you all the attention you deserve. That's why schedules are created, to make sure you get time with both your parents.

CHAPTER FOUR

WHEN YOU DON'T LIVE WITH EITHER PARENT

Sometimes after a divorce, neither parent is capable of caring for their children. In this case, when there are no other family members for them to live with, the children will go into foster care. Children all over the United States live in foster homes. A foster home may be a house or an apartment with two married foster parents or a single foster parent, and they may have other foster kids or kids of their own living there.

The state is responsible for children's welfare, and employees of state agencies decide if children need to be in foster care. The state agency that trains and licenses foster parents is usually Child Protective Services (CPS). CPS has the duty to investigate abuse, neglect, and abandonment cases. In most states, CPS provides services designed to help families solve their problems and stay together. One of these services is foster care.

Children whose parents can't care for them and who have no other relatives to live with may be placed in foster care. This situation can be temporary, until one of their parents is able to take them back.

Maggie's mother had come apart after Maggie's dad left the family last year. She started drinking a lot after Maggie and Maggie's little sister, Jade, had gone to bed. After she wrecked the car on the way to Jade's dance recital, Maggie's mother spent a few nights in the hospital. She took the pills she was prescribed for pain long after she needed them. Eventually she lost her waitressing job.

Maggie's mom seemed to stay in bed most of the time, so Maggie took care of Jade as best she could. She also had her homework to do, not to mention her part-time job washing dishes at the diner. By the time she got to school each day, she was exhausted. Her teachers noticed. They sent her to the guidance counselor, who talked to Maggie about her situation.

Soon after, a social worker came to the house and met with Maggie's mother, Maggie, and Jade. The girls were put in the custody of a foster care worker. They were told that they would be placed in foster homes until their mother could get her life back together.

The Need for Foster Care

Why would anybody take you out of your own home? Well, sometimes when parents get divorced, they find themselves unable to care for their kids. Depression is a fairly common side effect of divorce. Depression is a deep sense of sadness and unhappiness that lasts a long time. Some adults don't handle these feelings well or don't seek therapy when they need it. A few parents may turn to drugs or alcohol or may already have a substance abuse problem. Kids who need foster care come from families that need help. Their parents may have neglected, abandoned, or abused them physically or emotionally.

Neglect, the most common form of child abuse, can be physical, emotional, or educational. Parents may fail to supervise their children or make sure they get health care, food, clothing, or shelter. They may not make their children go to school. These are all good reasons to remove you from your parents' home and put you somewhere safe. None of them are your fault. Your parents may need professional help to recover from drug or alcohol abuse. Abusing drugs and alcohol makes it difficult to take care for oneself, let alone one's children.

Divorce is a traumatic experience that can drop a person into a deep depression. This might result in physical or emotional abuse of children. If this happens to you, talk to a trusted adult immediately.

Your parents may also have psychological or emotional problems that make them unable or unwilling to take care of their children. It's important for you to remember that no matter what anyone says, neglect is never your fault. It's not your job to make sure that your parents take proper care of you.

Why Would I Need Foster Care?

Child Protective Services depends quite a bit on responsible adults to protect the state's children. They need a responsible adult to tell them when there's a child that needs help. If you're in an unhealthy or dangerous situation at home, there are several things that can happen. You can ask for help yourself by talking to a trusted teacher, a school counselor, or a family friend. If you don't do this, but one of these people notices that there are problems in your home, he or she may call CPS to report suspected abuse. A social worker, someone who is trained to offer help to you and your family, will respond to the report. He or she will talk to the person who filed the complaint, your parents, and you.

The social worker's job is to determine the level of risk involved in allowing you to stay in your parents' home. Do your parents simply need a little help in taking care of you, or are they actually dangerous to you? Ultimately, the goal is to keep families together or to get them back together eventually. The social worker may decide that you can stay but also that your family requires services. Services could be counseling or parenting classes, among other things. However, if the social worker feels that it is in your best interest to remove you from your home, he or she will recommend it. If your parents agree with the social worker, he or she must take your case to juvenile, family, or probate court to discuss it with a judge. The judge will make the final decision about whether or not to remove you from the home. If the judge agrees with the social worker, the social worker will bring the court order to take you out of the home and place you with a foster family as quickly as possible.

If your parents refuse to allow the social worker to remove you, then the social worker will return with a police officer to get you out of the unsafe environment. In sexual abuse cases, the police officer that accompanies the social worker is specially trained to deal with victims of sexual abuse. This sounds like a scary situation, but it is important for you to keep in mind that the police officer and the social worker are not there to break up your family. They have come to make sure that you don't get hurt. Sometimes it is best for your family members to take a break from each other, particularly if a parent is treating you badly.

After you're placed in foster care, your case then goes from the social worker to a foster care worker. A foster care worker will work with your foster parents, your parents, and you to work out a contract. Parents are required to show by their actions that

FOSTER PARENTS

Not just anyone can be a foster parent. Foster parents are specially trained and licensed by Child Protective Services. They have to show they have certain qualities needed to be good foster parents. They must be responsible and stable and have patience and understanding. They must be willing to learn from the experience of being a foster parent. They have to have room in their lives to love foster children. They also have to be able to let them go when the time comes for them to return home.

Foster parents don't just need room in their lives for foster kids; they need room in their homes. They have to be able to give you a bedroom, or if you're sharing with another kid, one that's big enough for everybody. (The average foster parent is licensed to care for up to three children.) Their home should also be a safe, emotionally healthy place.

Foster parents can be married, single, or divorced. They can live in a house or an apartment. They can be as young as twenty-one years old and working outside the home, or they can be older, retired people. More and more often, the foster care system is turning to the relatives of children who need care to be providers of foster care. This type of foster care is called kinship care.

they intend to work to get you returned to them. They must solve whatever problem caused you to be in foster care. The contract is one in which all family members agree to accept whatever social services are required to reunite the family.

Am I Being Adopted?

Foster care and adoption are not the same thing. Adoption is a legal process through which an adult legally becomes the parent of someone who is not his or her biological child. If you are adopted, you are a permanent member of a new family, and your birth parents have no legal tie to you.

Ideally, foster care is temporary. Under certain circumstances, however, foster parents become adoptive parents. If your parents cannot care for you for an extended time, they can give up their legal rights to you.

Children in foster care are generally there only temporarily. The goal is to get your family back together or find a more permanent situation for you—especially if you have been in foster care for two years or more. Your stay in a foster home could be as short as overnight or as long as several years.

At the age of eighteen, you "age out" of foster care. This means that you must move on from the foster home, either by working and living on your own or with a member of your biological family or going to college. You will receive help with this process, and you will be able to talk to your case worker about any concerns that you may have. Unfortunately, this system is not the best it could be. The number of foster care agencies that provide employment-related services is limited. However, your high school may be very helpful in assisting you to find a job.

If you are adopted, your adoptive parents' responsibilities for you are the same as they would be for any biological child they have. They will help you with school and employment to the best of their abilities. Your care is up to them, not to Child Protective Services.

No matter whether you're placed with strangers or relatives, you will have a case worker whose job it is to look out for your welfare. That's whom you should talk to if you're having problems in your foster home you can't solve on your own. It will probably feel strange to move in with strangers, but as you get to know them, they'll feel more like family. Your foster family is there to help you and care for you. You can talk to them about things that are bothering you—your homework, your friends, or other problems—just as you would in a biological family.

CHAPTER FIVE

WHEN YOU NEED TO STAY AWAY FROM YOUR PARENTS

In some extreme, and extremely rare, cases, you might need to strike out on your own. It might be too dangerous to be around either of your parents. You might be old enough to take care of yourself. Perhaps the foster care system has failed you. For some teens who can prove they are able to survive on their own, legal emancipation is an option.

An emancipated minor is someone under the age of eighteen who is legally emancipated, or free from, his or her parents or guardian. You live apart from your parents; you're not receiving any financial support from them; and you're not in foster care. You can gain emancipation in several ways: you can go to court and ask a judge to order it; you can get married; or you can enlist in the armed services. There may also be other situations in which your state's laws allow emancipation.

In many states, enlisting in the armed forces after a certain age leads to automatic emancipation. Of course, this is a big commitment and should not be done without careful consideration.

Not all states allow minors to seek emancipation. If your state has such a law, you need to find out about it and follow its requirements. Then the court will hear your case and decide what's best for you. You may have to show that you have a job, that the job provides a salary with which you pay all your own bills, that you live in your own place, and that your parents aren't claiming you as a dependent on their taxes.

Karina had been living with her foster family, the Balduccis, for more than a year. She had moved in with them when officials discovered her father had been sexually abusing her. Karina's mother had abandoned them when Karina was little, and Karina had no idea where she was.

The Balduccis were so good to Karina that she thought of them as the family she'd always wanted. Together they discussed the idea of making Karina a permanent member of the family. Mr. and Mrs. Balducci wanted to adopt Karina, but they couldn't do that without the permission of Karina's parents.

Since Karina couldn't find her mother, and she certainly didn't feel safe with her father, she filed for legal emancipation. This would end any legal rights her parents could have over her. The court saw that emancipation and adoption by the Balduccis was in Karina's best interest.

Too Good to Be True?

Emancipation sounds like every teenager's dream, but there's a lot more to it than you may think. Being emancipated comes with some serious adult responsibilities. You have to be mature to handle these responsibilities. You are entirely accountable for your welfare. In some ways, this may sound like a lot of fun—you can stay up as late as you want, eat whatever you want, hang out with whichever friends you feel like. But it's not all fun, and you should consider your circumstances carefully.

Emancipation is a legal option meant for teenagers who are being abused and neglected or who have been in foster care for a long time and have had little to no contact with their real parents over that time. You'll have to take care of yourself even if you are not yet old enough to vote, buy property, or rent a car. Talk with somebody you really trust before deciding to go ahead

Legal emancipation is not as carefree as it may seem. Emancipated minors must be able to hold a job and pay for all of their expenses. You might be surprised at how much rent, transportation, utilities, and food cost.

and ask a court for emancipation. And if you are already emancipated, always talk to other adults when you're facing a new problem or situation you're not sure how to handle.

Not all emancipated teenagers are abused or in danger, however. For example, there are several well-known cases of child actors who become emancipated from their parents. These actors make enough money to support themselves and live on their own. These teens don't seek emancipation because they don't like their parents. They do so so that their parents don't have to be present on set and comply with the other labor laws that apply to child actors.

Many child actors, such as Drew Barrymore, have filed for emancipation from their parents. This is usually to avoid having to comply with certain laws regarding child labor or to assume control of their finances.

The Privileges of Emancipation

Different states have different laws governing emancipation and offer different rights and privileges. In California, for example, a minor who becomes emancipated has all of the following rights and privileges:

- to seek medical, dental, or psychiatric care, without parental consent, knowledge, or liability
- to enter into a binding contract (buying a car, getting a loan, etc.)
- to sue or be sued in his or her own name
- to make or revoke a will (a document that gives instructions about what to do with your property after your death)
- to establish a residence
- to enroll in a school or college

Depending on where you live, you may not have all these rights, however. For example, in New York, an emancipated minor is still required to get parental consent to get working papers (which are needed to get a job) and is limited in the kind of jobs he or she can hold. A minor cannot bring a lawsuit and must have an adult sue on his or her behalf. An emancipated minor cannot buy or sell real estate, and he or she must get parental consent for routine health care.

In New York, the minor's rights include the right to keep his or her own wages, the right to sue for financial support from the parents if they forced the youth to leave home, the right to establish a legal residence and attend school where he or she lives, and if necessary, the right to public benefits such as food stamps.

It's clear that your rights and privileges will be different from state to state, so you should investigate your state's emancipation laws. Seeking legal emancipation is a difficult process. Make sure that there are adults you can trust and talk to about the problems you're having. Your lawyer can answer your legal questions, but you'll need help to work out your issues with your family.

Just as it's the duty of the court to act in your best interests, it is your job to figure out what might be best for you. It requires a lot of maturity to make this decision and to live with it. However, if the safest thing for you is to be free of your parents' authority, then you should carefully consider emancipation.

CHAPTER SIX

WHEN YOUR PARENTS REMARRY

Just when you've adapted to your custody situation, you might find you need to make another change. This is because it's not uncommon for divorced parents to find love again. When another person enters your family, schedule adjustments might be needed.

If one or both of your parents gets married again, your custody arrangement might need to change. This is especially true if your stepparent has children because he or she has a custody schedule, too. Working out the custody arrangements in a blended family can be especially complicated because there are so many "moving parts"—so many different circumstances to account for.

Andre got nervous when his father married Patricia. Patricia had two kids of her own. They lived with Patricia and stayed with their father every weekend. Andre's arrangement with his dad was to visit him every weekend. That meant Andre

Your custody arrangement might change if one or both of your parents marry again. Adjusting to a new visitation schedule might be difficult, but remember, you've done it before. You will know better how to cope this time.

was staying with his father and Patricia during the only time they had to themselves. He wondered if he would feel like a third wheel. Or maybe his father would want to change his visitation schedule so that Andre stayed with him during the week, when his new stepsisters were there. Or maybe he would want Andre to stay away altogether since he had a new family now.

The Addition of a Stepparent

Your parents' dating may only begin to get your attention if, for instance, Mom brings a date along with her the day she's supposed to visit you. Hopefully, she has not surprised you with the extra company. But if she has, you need to find some private, quiet time to tell her how you feel about that. That visitation time is yours to spend with your parent. If you're uncomfortable, your mom needs to know that. She may not like hearing it, but she'll probably understand. She has other time she can spend with her new friend.

Sometimes, after your parents have been dating other people for a while, one or both of them may decide to get married. There isn't anything that can prepare you for the confusion of feelings that comes when a parent tells you he or she is marrying someone new. You may feel you're betraying your mother if you're happy for your father; you may feel as if you've lost your father to his new wife. Or you might not know what you feel.

That's all pretty normal, and you can talk to your parents about it. What's important is to talk about it calmly. All the feelings and emotions stirred up in you and your parents over such an event can make people react in fear and anger. Obviously that's not the best way to talk about things. Figure out what frightens you about the new arrangements (you may even want to write it down) and explain it to your parents. If something about it makes you angry, you can explain that, too.

The Benefits of a Blended Family

If your parent remarries, you'll then be part of a blended family. A blended family is one that includes stepparents, stepsiblings, or half siblings. Half siblings are brothers or sisters with whom you share only one biological parent instead of two.

Life in a blended family can be tricky. You have to get used to having new people as part of your family. You'll probably even have to get used to living with a new parent or new brothers or

Blended families rarely come together as seamlessly as the family on *The Brady Bunch*. However, with a little time and effort, your new family can be a source of strength and supoort.

sisters. It takes time to adjust to such a big change, so don't worry if it feels weird at first. After a while, you'll all gradually start to feel more and more like a family.

A blended family can add wonderful things to your life. A stepparent, for instance, can be another source of wisdom and guidance. Don't think of your new stepparent as someone trying to replace your parent. Instead, think of him or her as a wise family member who also wants the best for you. Stepsiblings can be wonderful additions to your family, as well. Maybe you've always wanted a younger sister, an older brother, or a sibling your own age, and now you have that person in your life.

It's not always easy to be a part of a blended family, and often it's very difficult. But most people agree that it's worth the struggle of adjusting to the new family members. For the rest of your life, you'll have more family members to support, encourage, and love you. Who wouldn't want that?

Going from Stepparent to Parent

The laws that govern stepparent adoptions are different from adoption laws for nonrelatives. If your custodial parent remarries, and your noncustodial parent doesn't visit you or support you in any way, there's a chance that your stepmom or stepdad can adopt you. Usually, the court will notify your noncustodial parent and then begin proceedings to terminate his or her parental rights. In other words, the court will work to remove you from your noncustodial parent's authority and responsibility. Once you've been adopted by your stepparent, you are legally his or her child. Unless one of your parents has died, a stepparent cannot adopt you without legal consent to the adoption by your biological parent.

Your stepparent isn't meant to replace a parent or replace you in your parent's life. Rather, he or she is just another member of your family who wants to help and support you. If your parent loves this person, chances are you will, too.

In most states, a stepparent can adopt you if the absent parent gives written, legal consent to the adoption. He or she can also adopt you if the absent parent's rights are terminated in court, if the absent parent abandoned you (left you uncared for), or if the other parent has abandoned you. Laws about abandonment are different from state to state, and you should research them thoroughly.

Happily, Cinderella is just a fairy tale. Your life is unlikely to be taken over by an evil stepmother and stepsisters. Like all the other parts of your parents' divorce you have had to deal with, this one may take some patience on your part. You may not like every person your parent dates, but your relationship with that parent lasts through anything. Together, you and your mom and dad, and even your stepmom and stepdad, can create a family life that—although different from the one you once had—can be filled with love and happiness.

GLOSSARY

ALIMONY Money that one parent may pay to the other after a divorce to help pay bills.

BLENDED FAMILY Family that includes stepparents, stepsiblings, or half siblings.

CHILD SUPPORT Money that the noncustodial parent pays to the custodial parent to help pay for the child's food, clothes, school, medical expenses, and other day-to-day costs.

CUSTODIAL PARENT The parent with whom the child lives.

CUSTODY The legal right and obligation to care for a child.

DEPENDENT Financially reliant on others.

DEPRESSION A deep sense of sadness and unhappiness that lasts a long time.

EMANCIPATED MINOR A person under the age of eighteen who is legally free from his or her parents or guardian.

FIXED VISITATION SCHEDULE A schedule of visits with the non-custodial parent that has been arranged by the court.

FOSTER CARE An arrangement in which a minor is placed with a foster family or in a group home.

GUARDIAN A person legally responsible for the welfare of another person.

IRRECONCILABLE DIFFERENCES Disagreements that cannot be solved.

JOINT LEGAL CUSTODY A legal arrangement in which parents share the authority over and responsibility for their child.

JOINT PHYSICAL CUSTODY A legal arrangement in which a child spends a more or less equal amount of time with each parent.

KINSHIP CARE Foster care in which the foster parent is a relative of the child in need of care.

MINOR A person under the age of eighteen.

MOTION A written request.

NO-FAULT DIVORCE A divorce that happens simply because of the couple's inability to get along with each other.

NONCUSTODIAL PARENT The parent who has visitation rights; the child doesn't live with this parent.

SOCIAL WORKER A person specially trained to offer counseling services and other help to families in trouble.

SOLE LEGAL CUSTODY A legal arrangement in which one parent makes all the decisions about the child's day-to-day life.

STIPULATED MODIFICATION A change to a visitation or to the custody arrangement, made with the agreement of both parents but independent of the court.

TERMINATE To bring to an end.

VISITATION RIGHTS Legal privilege given to the noncustodial parent to see his or her child regularly.

FOR MORE INFORMATION

Administration for Children and Families
330 C Street SW
Washington, DC 20201
Website: https://www.acf.hhs.gov
The Administration for Children and Families (ACF) promotes
the economic and social well-being of families, children,
individuals, and communities with partnerships, funding,
guidance, training, and technical assistance.

American Association for Marriage and Family Therapy
112 South Alfred Street
Alexandria, VA 22314-3061
(703) 838-9808
Website: http://www.aamft.org
This organization offers support and suggestions for seeking
family therapy to cope with divorce and blended families.

Childhelp USA Hotline
(800) 422-4453
This hotline is available in English and Spanish for young people in crisis.

Children's Rights Council
1296 Cronson Boulevard
Suite 3086
Crofton, MD 21114
(301) 459-1220
Website: http://www.crckids.org
The Children's Rights Council is dedicated to helping divorced,
separated, and never-married parents remain actively and

responsibly involved in their children's lives. Parents can join local groups to help them deal with their situation.

Erika's Lighthouse
897 1/2 Green Bay Road
Winnetka, IL 60093
(847) 386-6481
Website: http://www.erikaslighthouse.org
This organization educates and empowers teens to take charge of their mental health.

Legal Information for Families Today (LIFT)
32 Court Street, Suite 1208
Brooklyn, NY 11201
(646) 613-9633
Website: http://www.liftonline.org/programs /resources-children-and-teens
The mission of LIFT is to enhance access to justice for children and families by providing legal information, community education, and compassionate guidance, while promoting system-wide reform of the courts and public agencies.

Office of the Cook County Public Guardian
2245 W. Ogden Avenue, 4th Floor
Chicago, IL 60612
(312) 433-4300
Website: http://www.publicguardian.org/juvenile/youth -resources/youth-advocacy-post-emancipation
This bureau provides practical advice to teens seeking emancipation in the Chicago area. It also places teens with caregivers and acts as an advocate for teens.

Stepfamily Foundation
310 West 85th St. Suite 1B
New York, NY 10024
(212) 877-3244
Website: http://www.stepfamily.org
This nonprofit organization provides counseling for the step-
family/blended family, divorce counseling, remarriage
counseling, and stepfamily certification seminars.

Websites

Because of the changing nature of Internet links, Rosen Publishing has developed an online list of websites related to the subject of this book. This site is updated regularly. Please use this link to access this list:

http://www.rosenlinks.com/DIV/custody

FOR FURTHER READING

Baker, Amy J. L., and Katherine Andre. *Getting Through My Parents' Divorce*. Oakland, CA: Instant Help Books, 2015.

Bergin, Rory M., and Jared Meyer. *Frequently Asked Questions About Divorce*. New York, NY: Rosen Publishing, 2012.

Bryfonski, Dedria. *Child Custody*. Farmington Hills, MI: Greenhaven Press, 2011.

Espejo, Roman. *Custody and Divorce*. Detroit, MI: Greenhaven Press, 2013.

Gay, Kathlyn. *Divorce: The Ultimate Teen Guide*. Lanham, MD: Rowman & Littlefield, 2014.

Hudson, David L. *Child Custody Issues*. New York: Chelsea House, 2012.

Iorizzo, Carrie. *Divorce and Blended Families*. St. Catharines, Ontario: Crabtree Publishing Company, 2013.

Kavanaugh, Dorothy. *Hassled Girl? Girls Dealing with Feelings*. Berkeley Heights, NJ: Enslow Publishers, 2014.

McLaughlin, Jerry, and Katherine E. Krohn. *Dealing with Your Parents' Divorce*. New York, NY: Rosen Publishing, 2016.

Peterman, Rosie L., Jared Meyer, and Charlie Quill. *Divorce and Stepfamilies*. New York, NY: Rosen Publishing, 2013.

Prentzas, G. S. *The Law and Your Family: Your Legal Rights*. New York, NY: Rosen Publishing, 2015.

Stewart, Sheila, and Rae Simons. *I Live in Two Homes: Adjusting to Divorce and Remarriage*. Broomall, PA: Mason Crest Publishers, 2011.

INDEX

A

abandonment, 33, 35, 43, 54

abuse, 23, 25, 33, 35, 37, 43, 44
  emotional, 10, 35
  physical, 10, 35
  sexual, 37, 42–43

adoption, 39–40, 43
  stepparent, 52, 54

alcohol abuse, 10, 25, 30, 35

alimony, 9

B

bird's nest custody, 18

blended families, 48
  benefits of, 50, 52

C

case worker, 40

Child Protective Services (CPS),
    33, 36, 37, 38, 40

child support, 9, 26

court system, 6, 9, 13, 14, 18, 20,
    23, 25–26, 37, 41, 42, 43–44,
    47, 52, 54
  approval by, 30
  custody decisions made by,
    9–10, 12, 18, 20, 23, 26

custodial parent, 8–9, 23, 25, 28,
    29, 30, 31, 52
  job of, 26
  schedule of, 26

custody

arrangements in a blended
    family, 48

definition, 6

modification of, 30, 48

options, 6, 7–8, 10, 13, 14, 15,
    17, 18, 20, 23

process for deciding, 6, 9, 14,
    22, 23

D

depression, 35

divorce
  definition of, 4
  effect on children, 4–6
  emotions around, 5, 6, 28, 35
  rearrangement of family after, 4,
    14, 32, 54
  statistics on, 4

drug abuse, 10, 25, 28, 30, 35

E

emancipation, of minors, 41–44
  laws regarding, 46, 47
  privileges of, 46

emotions, 5, 6, 50

F

fixed visitation schedule, 23

foster care, 33, 39, 40, 41, 43
  agencies, 40
  failure of system, 41
  need for, 35–38
  workers, 38

About the Authors

Timothy Callahan is a teacher and writer who lives in Pittsburgh, Pennsylvania.

Claudia Isler was born and raised in New York City. She has edited material ranging in subject from robotic engineering to soap operas.

Photo Credits

Cover Lisa F. Young/Shutterstock.com; back cover, pp. 4–5 © iStockphoto .com/jsmith; p. 5 Echo/Getty Images; p. 8 BananaStock/Thinkstock; p. 11 Serg Zastavkin/Shutterstock.com; pp. 12–13 © Marmaduke St. John/ Alamy Stock Photo; p. 16 Blend Images/Ariel Skelley/Getty Images; p. 19 Fuse/Getty Images; p. 21 © iStockphoto.com/Erik Khalitov; p. 24 Andersen Ross/Blend Images/Thinkstock; p. 25 © MBI/Alamy Stock Photo; p. 27 © iStockphoto.com/harreha; p. 31 © Tetra Images/Alamy Stock Photo; p. 34 fstop123/E+/Getty Images; p. 36 Peter Dazeley/Photographer's Choice/Getty Images; p. 39 Gone Wild/Taxi/Getty Images; p. 42 © iStockphoto.com/car- lofranco; p. 44 Inti St. Clair/DigitalVision/Getty Images; p. 45 Steve Granitz/ WireImage/Getty Images; p. 49 © iStockphoto.com/JGould; p. 51 © AF archive/Alamy Stock Photo; p. 53 Eric Audras/Onoky/Getty Images; interior pages textured background chungking/Shutterstock.com.

Designer: Nicole Russo; Editor: Christine Poolos;
Photo Researcher: Karen Huang